Bear's Birthday

Allan Ahlberg

Colin McNaughton

Bear's Birthday
Big Head
Open the Door

RANDOM HOUSE 🏠 NEW YORK

First American Edition, 1986.
Copyright © 1985 by Walker Books Ltd. All rights
reserved under International and Pan-American Copyright
Conventions. Published in the United States by Random
House, Inc., New York. Originally published in Great Britain by
Walker Books Ltd., London.

Library of Congress Cataloging in Publication Data: Ahlberg, Allan. Bear's birthday. (Red nose
readers) SUMMARY: Labeled pictures demonstrate meanings of open and shut and happy and
sad in vignettes featuring aggressive monsters and a bear's
birthday party. [1. Vocabulary]
I. McNaughton, Colin.   II. Title.   III. Series: Ahlberg, Allan. Red nose readers.
PE1449.A34   1985   428.1   84-27746
ISBN: 0-394-87197-9 (trade); 0-394-97197-3 (lib. bdg.)

Manufactured in Singapore

1 2 3 4 5 6 7 8 9 0

Bear's
Birthday

a bear

a happy bear

a happy birthday bear

a happy birthday bear
and his friends

a party

a happy party

a happy noisy party

a sad noisy party

a sad noisy bear

a happy bear

tickle
tickle

a happy ending

Big
Head

big head

little head

big ear

little ear

big eye   little eye

big nose   little nose

big mouth

little mouth

little hat

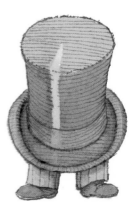

big hat

Open
the
Door

open the door

close the door

open the window

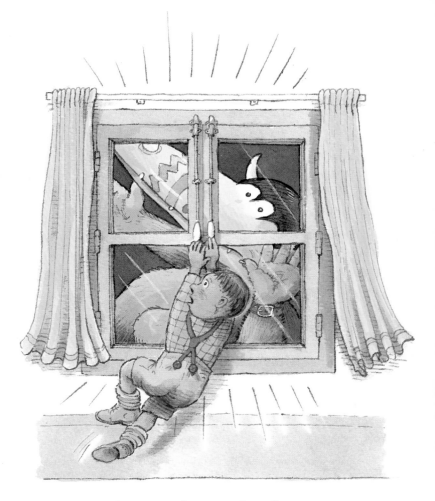

close the window

open the fridge

close the fridge

open the box

close the box

open the package